Snakes

Kate Riggs

CREATIVE EDUCATION

seedlings

Published by Creative Education
P.O. Box 227, Mankato, Minnesota 56002
Creative Education is an imprint of
The Creative Company
www.thecreativecompany.us

Design by Ellen Huber
Production by Chelsey Luther
Art direction by Rita Marshall
Printed in the United States of America

Photographs by 123rf (Eric Chiang), Dreamstime (Amwu,
Sarel Van Staden), iStockphoto (Eric Isselée, Ian McDonnell,
OldGreyMan, webphotographeer), National Geographic
Stock (LUIS ESPIN), Shutterstock (Eric Isselée, Heiko Kiera,
mikeledray, Patries, Robynrg, B. Stefanov, Arie v.d. Wolde),
SuperStock (Corbis, Minden Pictures)

Library of Congress Cataloging-in-Publication Data
Riggs, Kate.
Snakes / Kate Riggs.
p. cm. — (Seedlings)
Includes index.
Summary: A kindergarten-level introduction to snakes,
covering their growth process, behaviors, the habitats
they call home, and such defining physical features as
their scaly skin.
ISBN 978-1-60818-343-2
1. Snakes—Juvenile literature. I. Title.

QL666.O6R45 2013
597.96—dc23   2012023425

First Edition
9 8 7 6 5 4 3 2 1

TABLE OF CONTENTS

Hello, snakes!

Snakes are animals
called reptiles.

They live all around the world.

Snakes have scales that cover their bodies.

They do not
have arms
or legs.

Snakes can be
big or little.

All snakes have forked tongues.

Snakes eat meat. Some snakes eat mice and frogs. Other snakes eat deer!

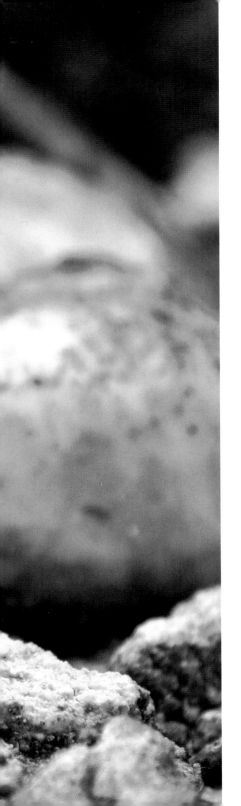

A baby snake comes out of an egg. Or it is born live. Baby snakes grow up by themselves.

Snakes like to lie around in the sun. Then they look for food.

Goodbye, snakes!

Picture a Snake

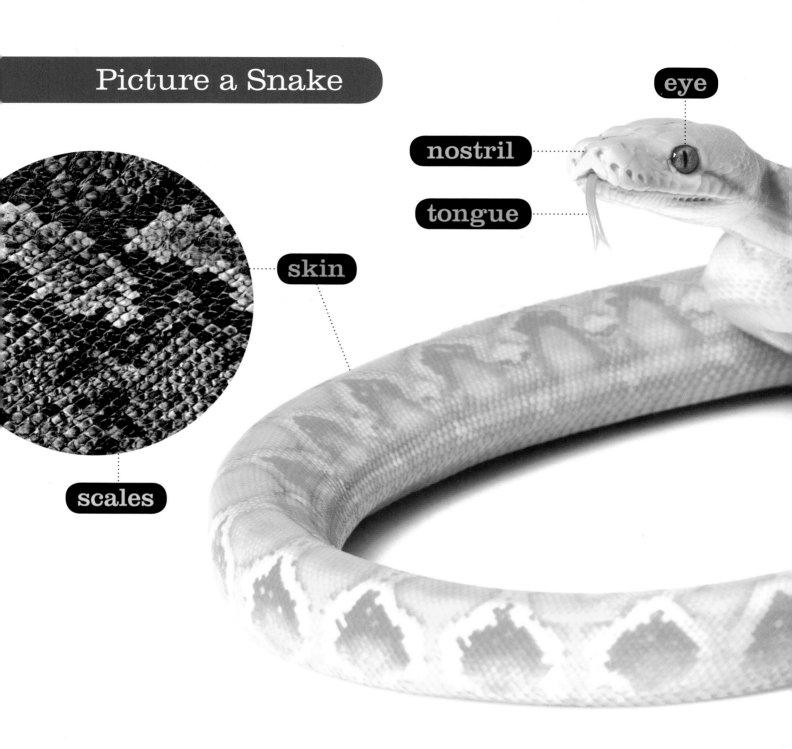

eye

nostril

tongue

skin

scales

fang

jaws

tail

Words to Know

forked: split into two parts

reptiles: animals that have scales and need heat from the sun to keep warm

scales: small, bony plates that cover an animal's skin

Read More

Stewart, Melissa. *Snakes.*
Washington, D.C.: National Geographic Society, 2009.

Thomson, Sarah L. *Amazing Snakes!*
New York: HarperCollins, 2006.

Websites

DLTK's Snake Activities
http://www.dltk-kids.com/animals/snakes.htm
Make a snake craft. Or print out pictures to color.

Snake Activities
http://www.kidzone.ws/lw/snakes/activities.htm
Learn more about snakes by doing puzzles and coloring
booklets.

Index